Message in a bottle

Message
in a
Bottle

selected poems

Ann M. Schultz

Ann Schultz

ARTPACKS • ROCHESTER

Published by Artpacks
Rochester, Minnesota 55906
507-273-2529
storymatters@charter.net

Publishing, fine art printing, and studio workshops in book arts
and life development

Contact Artpacks to order copies of *Message in a Bottle*
Checks, Mastercard and VISA are accepted
Shipping and handling charges are $3 per book

Printed in the United States of America

Library of Congress Cataloging-in-Publication Data
Schultz, Ann M., 1917-
  Message in a Bottle : selected poems / Ann M. Schultz.
     p. cm.
  ISBN 978-0-9790247-9-5 (pbk. : alk. paper)
  I. Title.
  PS3619.C477M47 2010
  811'.6--dc22

                                        2010021472

To my family

CONTENTS

INTRODUCTION

FAMILY AND CHILDREN

HOME AND GARDEN

AFTER THOUGHTS

Introduction

It was not until her late forties that my mother, Ann Schultz, discovered her gift of poetry. Repeated bouts of pneumonia had left her with partially paralyzed vocal cords, a weak voice, difficult breathing, and a chronic lung disease which makes talking exhausting and has restricted her activities since then.

After speech therapy at the Mayo Clinic did not result in much improvement, she discovered that she could express her thoughts in poetry better than verbally and began writing her observations in verse.

She has written over two hundred poems, many humorous, some poignant, and others religious, all perceptive and thought-provoking. When my husband, Ken, reads Mother's poems to groups, they evoke both tears and chuckles, and people always want to hear more.

Mother's first published poem, "Were You There?" appeared in *The Methodist Woman* in March of 1965. The second was "Carpe Diem," featured in *Chatelaine* in September of 1976. Since then she has had many poems published and has received many rejection slips. Undaunted, she continues to submit her work to editors of magazines, often with positive results.

As a family, we have always looked forward to Mother's latest creations, occasionally suggesting subjects. Our dad used to say that when Mother couldn't sleep at night, there would be new poems in the morning.

My sister, Roberta, once told Mother that she should not be hiding her poems in a dresser drawer like Emily Dickinson. With Mother's permission, Roberta then set out to type and gather them in three-ring binders for family members. Many she illustrated with pictures cut out of magazines. Roberta continued to add new poems to our books until her untimely death early in 2004, when I took over the task.

Now at ninety-two and in frail health, Mother is still writing and getting her work published. In a very real sense, her poetry has given back to her and to us the voice she lost more than forty years ago. For that we are grateful.

For our family and friends, Mother is an inspiration, living well with a chronic illness while continuing to use her gifts and find purpose.

Read, savor, and enjoy!

Janet Panger

MESSAGE IN A BOTTLE

Family and Children

Carpe Diem

It's too much trouble to go to the beach
We'll wait for another day
When the floors are scrubbed and the clothes are washed
And everything put away.

It's hot at the beach and the flies are out
And I have an aching head.
So we stayed at home, and to make it up
I bought them a toy instead.

And then one day my work was done.
"Let's go to the beach," I said,
And I looked outside, but the wind was cold
And summer's leaves were red.

And I looked around for those golden heads
But the children too had flown.
And I know that now if I go at all
I'll go to the beach alone.

Grandchild

There wasn't time to do the things I dreamed,
Long autumn walks, slow summers in the sun,
Time to look and listen, time to play
Work and worry stole the years away.

But now once more a little hand finds mine
And young eyes teach my own again to see.
Oh, miracle, oh blessed second chance,
The child you were come back again to me.

First Gift

The flowers you sent today were beautiful
But I must tell you this – please understand
No flowers have ever thrilled me like that first bouquet
Of dandelions in a chubby little hand.

Lost Moment

She came with shining eyes on dancing feet
To share some childish joy or wonder why.
But, being occupied with grown-up things,
"Don't interrupt. I'm busy now," I said.
"We'll talk about it later when I'm free."

Why should I wonder that she turned away
With downcast eyes, the magic moment gone,
Or be surprised that later never came?

Adolescence

Just yesterday your eyes were wide with wonder
At rocks and sticks and puddles on our street.
Now we show you oceans, forests, mountains,
And your response? "Hey, Mom, when do we eat?"

Nostalgia

Our winter landscape, once the site
Of building projects grand
And snowball fights and games of pie
Now wears an aspect bland.

Our snow, once cut in blocks to build
Or molded, trampled, piled,
Now lies in undisturbed repose,
Smooth, white, and undefiled.

Then one day a welcome sight
From winters long ago –
A group of neighbor children
Making angels in our snow.

Home and Garden

No Losers Here

Estate sales are a little sad
They're held when someone dies,
And treasures of a life are spread
Before uncaring eyes.

Garage sales, on the other hand,
Have all the fun and flair
Of medieval marketplace
Bazaar or county fair.

One neighbor cleans her closets
And gains some needed space.
Another finds a treasure
To adorn an empty place.

And everyone is happy.
You can see it by their grins
It's one of those rare business deals
Where everybody wins.

Garage Sales

Garage sales lift my spirits
Because it's there I find
That other people's cast off junk
Is even worse than mine.

Rite of Spring

Spring cleaning. Is there anyone
Who does it anymore?
Cleans the cupboards, empties drawers
Scrubs every inch of floor?

No, this peculiar ritual
No more has devotees
To propagate its holy writ
And worship on their knees.

The priestesses have left the shrine.
The sacred fires burn low.
When paid employment beckons
What can they do but go?

Mother Nature Knows Best

Let your grass go dormant
Follow nature's way.
Fall rains will bring it back to life.
At least that's what they say.

So I let my grass go dormant
'Til it crunched beneath my tread
And now that the fall rains have come
It's still dormant – more like dead.

Sudden Death

My neighbor's grass is sleek and groomed.
Mine grows wild and free.
No dandelions mar her sod.
She has ChemLawn, you see.

My lawn is an eclectic mix
Of grasses wild and tame
And dandelions and other weeds
Too numerous to name.

But every year when spring rolls 'round
There comes a sweet surprise –
A purple haze of violets
For winter-weary eyes.

They came one day when I was out.
(They had the wrong address.)
They sprayed my yard with 2-4D
And killed the violets.

Back to Nature

My weed infested sod was once
A source of great chagrin.
I viewed my neighbor's velvet lawn
And knew I'd never win
The constant war with noxious weeds
That sprouted everywhere.
I put away my weed digger
And gave up in despair.

But now we hear a bright new note
Ringing loud and clear
From the environmentalists
Who seldom bring us cheer
That now it's chic to have a lawn
Where native plants grow free.
It even has a fancy name,
Biodiversity.

Let Nature Rule

Naturalize your lawn they say
Let native plants grow free
Make your yard a welcome home
For squirrel and bird and bee.

Put away your weed digger
Let dandelions take over
Encourage quack and crab grass
Grow fragrant fields of clover.

Your neighbors may not like it
Their complaints may be emphatic
But don't let that discourage you
The birds will be ecstatic.

Sounds of Summer

My air conditioner supplies
Fresh air in scientific quantities.
But, oh, I miss the music of birds' cries
The soft swish of breezes through the trees.

Art on the Windowpane

Our homes are well protected
From winter's frigid blasts
Our windows tight and thermopaned
No frost invades our glass.

And though we're snug and cozy warm
Yet something has been lost
Remember how we loved to find
Pictures in the frost?

Those lacy, feathery landscapes
No artist could devise
A magic scene from fairyland
Delighted wondering eyes.

Our glass is clear. Our view improved
And yet we mourn the loss
Of winter's icy fingers drawing
Pictures in the frost.

Education

To a Teacher

Teacher, if you only knew
The hope and trust we place in you
As we let go this trembling hand
Teacher, you'd be trembling too.

Be gentle with this little child
He's only five, you know
And though he has matured a lot
He still has far to go.

Walk softly through his wakening mind
Open the windows wide
Take his hand and lead him
To the wondrous world outside.

Give him heroes to admire
Wise words to stretch his mind
Feed his imagination
With story, song, and rhyme.

Send him proudly home each day
With something new to tell.
He's yours for this brief time
We hope and pray you'll use it well.

The First Day of School

I left my child at school today,
Walked home on leaden feet.
His little chin was trembling
As he went to take his seat.

The teacher was so very young.
How could she understand
The lump that would not swallow down
As I let go his hand.

I've planned ahead. I've done my best
To bring him to this day.
I never thought he'd be the one
To drag his feet and say,
"Mom, I don't want to go to school.
I'll just stay home and play."

The morning drags; my work all done
In half the usual time
I nervously repeat each task,
Await the noonday chime.

Then – running feet. The door slams shut.
A voice rings like a bell.
My son runs laughing to my arms.
"Hey Mom, my teacher's swell."

A DNA test for pre-schoolers has
been developed that predicts what
sports they will excel in.

Parent Alert!

Line up your toddlers, parents
There's now a test to tell
In which of all the sports
Your little athlete will excel.

Why should he waste his precious time
On games he likes to play
When he could be in training
For a spot in the NBA?

Athletic scholarships are scarce
And competition keen
It's not too early to prepare
For that prestigious team.

Pre-school

Strap on your backpack, little one
There's no more time for play.
Put away your dolls and toys
Your color crayons and clay.

You're training for the workforce now
Though you are only three
Say goodbye to fun and games
And such frivolity.

If you should find it hard to pass
Those math and science tests
Tutors are available
To help you do your best.

Assignment

"I did the best I could," she said, and hung her head.
I knew she spoke the truth, could picture well
The slow and patient struggle that produced
This blotted page. I felt a sudden shame.
How many times in all my teaching years
Could I have truthfully made such a claim?

Phonics or Fonicks – or Fonix?

Teach our children phonics
Or they'll never learn to read.
Make them sound each letter
Or their progress you'll impede.

There's just one problem with this plan
And its advocates frenetic.
Of all the languages on earth
Ours is the least phonetic.

How to explain to little ones
Bought, caught, not, and knot?
Or clarify the reason why
Thought is not spelled thot?

If older folks were in the mood
To do some frank confessing
They'd say they learned our language
By some very clever guessing.

What's in a Name?

Creative math is nothing new
It's been here all along.
But what's now dubbed creative
Was once called plain dead wrong.

The Child Speaks

Don't accelerate me, please
I need more time to play.
You'd be surprised how much I learn
Something new each day.

This big wide world is new to me
I need time to explore
And that strange language that you speak
Each day I de-code more.

So talk, and sing and read to me
I'll learn at my own rate
Whatever other parents do
Please don't accelerate.

Cultural Diversity

To learn of other cultures
Is a worthy aim it's true
But in our zeal let's not forget
We have a culture too.

Second Thoughts

Admonition

When someone tramps with careless feet
On what we hold most dear
Dismisses our most cherished dream
With scornful wounding sneer
We may not show the hurt we feel
We're friendly as before
But somewhere deep within our hearts
We close and lock a door.
Tread softly when another dreams
Respect what once you mocked
Or someday you may knock and find
All doors are closed and locked.

Snowflakes

The snow falls softly on the ground
And gently on my face
And decorates my somber clothes
With filigrees of lace.

Serious Business

I see the joggers sprinting by
Mile after healthful mile.
They look athletic, fit, and strong
But I've yet to see one smile.

Embarrassing Question

When other people bore me
So I almost want to cry
A troubling question comes to mind –
How interesting am I?

Social Savoir Faire

Some people know just what to do
In every situation
The words to say, the gift to send.
They earn our admiration.

The rest of us just muddle through
Without such expertise
Just hoping that somehow we'll make
More friends than enemies.

A Word to the Wise

Decision making skills are good.
They serve us well in life's events.
But here's advice that's tried and true
When all else fails try common sense.

"The Greatest of These Is Charity"

With people who are critical
We're never quite at ease
We never know just what to say
Or what to do to please.

With others we can be ourselves
Confident and free
Knowing what we do or say
Is judged with charity.

I Wonder

When people start to criticize
Their friends unmercifully
I wonder when I leave the room
What do they say of me?

Fallen Heroes

Washington and Jefferson
Once held a place secure
A grateful country offered them
A love that would endure.

Historians stalk the pantheon
Unveiling feet of clay
We'd have no heroes to admire
If they could have their way.

With patient diligence they probe
Each word, split every hair
But who'll replace our heroes when
Their pedestals are bare?

"Time Makes Ancient Good Uncouth"

They've just revised our hymn book
To bring it up to code.
They've overhauled the rhetoric
To fit the modern mode.

Like the inquisitors of old
They've scanned each word and text.
To root out hidden heresy
Of culture, creed, or sex.

It's not the hymns they've added
That fill us with dismay
But those that in their wisdom
They've seen fit to take away.

No more do Christian soldiers march
To win for Christ the day.
We can't have martial images
To lead our youth astray.

They've done away with Whittier's
Fine hymn, "0 Brother Man."
"God Rest Ye Merry Gentlemen"
Did not survive the ban.

Our good gray poet Lowell
Failed to pass the test.
His "Once to Every Man and Nation"
Was purged with all the rest.

They've left out all our favorites
To make our book more mod.
They've robbed us of our heritage.
Rise up, 0 folks of God!

Waste and Want

With faces pinched and hunger-widened eyes
And bodies weak with fever and privation
The starving children lift their empty bowls
While we throw out enough to feed a nation.

Viewer Discretion Advised

Polite circumlocution
Is no longer de rigueur.
We've all grown more enlightened,
More broad-minded, more secure.

The one last euphemism
We're required to endure
Is the one that coyly labels
Plain vulgarity "mature."

Roots

We stand apart like trees in woods,
Reach out to touch and find
That underneath the surface
Our roots are intertwined.

After Thought

At funerals we hear the best
No unkind words are said
We hear how wonderful he was
Now that our friend is dead.

But then around the edges
A chilling thought creeps in
Did that good person ever know
How well we thought of him?

Say It

If you have something good to say
Of anyone, just say it now
Don't wait to find the proper time and place
The proper card to send, the well turned phrase.
We never know when one kind word can help
A weary fellow traveler on the way
Just say it – now.

Appreciation

When the doctors work their miracles and leave
Who keeps the long night watch beside our bed?
Who soothes our aching bones with healing hands
And helps us find again the gift of sleep?

Who tries to comfort when we mourn the loss
Of health and strength or precious body part
And treats respectfully our nakedness?
With firm insistence guides our first weak steps
Toward recovery, knows when to push
And when to give support, and finally
Sends us on our way with hope renewed
Encouraged, strengthened to begin again.

Random Reflections

Beaver Spare that Tree

The beaver is a gentle beast
We admire his industry.
But he has one nasty habit.
He's cutting down our trees.

For the environmentalists
This is a quandary
Because they love the beaver, but
They also love the tree.

The most humane solution posed
For this perplexity
Is to sterilize the beaver,
Curtail his family.

But this is unacceptable.
Just think, it's very clear
His family values are at stake.
We dare not interfere.

Food Chain

The food chain, nature's answer
To the what's for dinner riddle.
How pleasant to be at the end
Instead of in the middle.

Packaging

Who was the clever person
Who invented all this trouble?
Each item that we buy encased
In a rock-hard plastic bubble!

Easy Open Package

At the top of my list of people
Whose ways I would like to amend
Is the one who prints small
On the box I just mangled
"Please open the other end."

Left-handed Lament

The person I'm longing to meet
The person I'm dreaming of
The person who'd meet my great need is the one
Who wears out the right rubber glove.

Letter Perfect

I love my spelling checker.
It almost never fails,
Except when there's this problem
Is it folk-tails or folk-tales?

Or complement or compliment
Lead or led, leach or leech?
Such fine discriminations
Are far beyond its reach.

I love my spelling checker.
Most errors it will find.
There's just one thing it cannot do.
It cannot reed my mind.

Creative Bookkeeping

I faithfully record each check.
Subtract them carefully
So when the statement comes, why don't
The bank and I agree?

Good Housekeeping

It's true, I have it on the very
Best authority
You only have to dust the things
Your tallest guest can see.

But sad to say, this sage advice
Affects me not at all
Because unluckily for me
My guests are always tall.

Concert Hall Syndrome

Why is it that at concerts
When the music's playing soft
The audience is stricken with
An urgent need to cough?

It starts with just one person,
But it soon becomes endemic.
Before long we're confronted with
A full-blown epidemic.

The cure's so obvious it's strange
It's not been tried before –
Ushers armed with free cough drops
Stationed near the door.

Informality Plus

Informality is nice
It puts us at our ease
And members of the waiting staff
Are trying hard to please.

But somehow when we're dining out
It comes as a surprise
When a charming waitress greets us with
These words, "How are you guys?"

Tolerance

I try to keep an open mind
Put prejudice to rout.
However, not so open
That my brains will all fall out.

The Fit Shall Inherit – or Your BMI Is Showing

Fitness now is paramount
Employers cast an eye
Not just on how you do your job
But what's your BMI.

Rewards and punishments abound
For the faithful employee –
Rewards for those who exercise
And eat their broccoli.

But those who do not rise at dawn
And join the fitness race
Might someday come to work and find
They've lost their parking space.

For those who might be tempted
For one moment to relax
A treadmill desk has been designed
To get them back on track.

The lunchroom menu has been changed
It's geared to fitness too.
Instead of hamburgers and fries
It's bean sprouts and tofu.

The coffee break has disappeared
The workout takes its place.
The cozy lounge is gone. A gym
Occupies its space.

The office is a different place
Since fitness came along
Inhabited by employees
Slender, fit, and strong.

So if you've been refused a job
Don't ask the reason why
It's not that you're unqualified
It's just your BMI.

Wisdom from the Past

Ancient Wisdom Re-visited

Look before you leap, of course.
All prudent people do it.
But look too long and you will find
Someone will beat you to it.

        No moss will ever gather
        On a rolling stone, we're told.
        But who wants moss, I wonder?
        It's second kin to mold.

The early bird will get the worm.
This much we know is true,
But think about it, it's quite clear
The worm was early too.

The First Shall Be Last

First things first they tell us
Good advice it's true,
But if I do the first things first
That's all I ever do.

Creativity

Necessity fosters invention, they say.
Here's one ancient saying that's true.
If there'd always been plenty of meat to go 'round
Do you think we'd have ever had stew?

The Hand that Rocks the Cradle

"The hand that rocks the cradle
is the hand that rules the world."

— W. R. Wallace

Few people doubt the wisdom
Of this venerable quote
But the hand that rules the household
Is the hand on the remote.

Question

I've thought about it often.
Will someone tell me why
A watched pot never boils
But an unwatched pot boils dry.

Advice

When people give us good advice
We're tempted to resent
An age-old saying comes to mind,
"Take kindly what is kindly meant."

Thoughts on Aging

Getting the Message

Young people raise their voices.
(They think I cannot hear.)
Explain things in the simplest terms.
They even call me "dear."

Small things, but they deliver
A message clear and bold
That even though I still feel young
I'm really getting old.

Voices from the Past

Our elders often bore us
With tales of days long gone
Battles fought, hardships endured
Great causes lost and won.

We struggle to suppress a yawn
Make an excuse to flee
Not knowing what we're tuning out
Is living history.

Be Patient

Be patient with me. I am growing old
And if you've heard my stories more than once
Listen anyway. And if my mind
Seems slow to grasp your meaning give me time.
My ears don't pick up every word you say.
My mind is not as nimble as it was.
And though my voice is weak, I still have need
For conversation, sharing thoughts with you.
I'm proud of what I did and what I was.
And so be patient. I will do the same.

Communication

Come sit beside me. There's no need to talk.
There's too much noisy chatter in this world.
It makes me sad to see how hard you try
To make me hear. Just sit here, touch my hand.

Together we'll enjoy this tranquil place,
We cannot hear the rustle of the leaves
Or bird song softly calling from the trees.

But if we listen, maybe we will hear
The whisper of that quiet inner voice
That brings us closer to the mind of God.

A Weary Nursing Home Resident Contemplates Heaven

Is there a rec director there
To keep us moving when we want to rest?
To put our minds and muscles to the test?
And if we don't take part we fall from grace
If so, I'd like to try the other place.

More Blessed

To give is gratifying
It boosts our self-esteem
And it's more blessed we are told
To meet another's need.

But sometimes it's more blessed
Although hard to believe
To put aside our foolish pride
And graciously receive.

Strife and Violence

Argument

Does it matter who's right and who's wrong?
Is it worth it to fight to the end?
Is it better to add one more notch to your gun,
Or better to keep a dear friend?

The Other Cheek?

"He hit me first," my little son declared
Bloody from schoolyard battlefield one day.
How could I say as I have often said,
"It takes a bigger man to walk away."

Middle East

When did it start? Was it when Abraham
Cast Ishmael out to die on desert sand?
His first born son robbed of his heritage
To please a jealous wife. Arab and Jew
Locked together in eternal strife
Each one bestowed the gift of promised land
Each looking back to Father Abraham.

Or was it when the Jews were Pharaoh's slaves
Or later when they wept in Babylon?
Or when crusaders came with fire and sword
To take back holy land they thought was theirs?
Or when the western powers carved up the land
Unmindful of its tortured history
Expecting ancient enemies to live
In harmony together side by side
Reopening old wounds that never healed.
When did it start? And will it ever end?

Lame Excuse

When nations stand before the throne of God
To learn what punishment their sins will fit
Will He be merciful when each one says,
With look of innocence, "They started it."

Fences or Bridges

We build our fences higher
Use every strategem
To fortify the barriers
That divide us from them.

Secure behind our barricades
We live and work and hide.
Their problems are not ours, we say
Two cities side by side.

But now our quiet streets explode
With violence and hate.
The problems we refused to face
Are knocking at our gate.

When will we learn that we must build,
Before our country falls,
Bridges instead of fences
Ladders instead of walls.

Political Commentary

Advice to a Politician

The tape recorder's running.
Be careful what you say.
Remember that the media
Will play it back someday.

Promises Promises

We'll give you everything you want
Bring peace, grind all your axes
And balance that sick budget too
And never raise your taxes.

Retribution

"The mills of the gods grind slowly
but they grind exceeding fine."

— S. Empiricus

We drove them off and took their land
Gave them the reservation.
We thought they'd never learn our ways
Adopt civilization.

Now their casinos dot the land
Spreading like a rash.
Now that at last they've learned our ways
They're taking all our cash.

Latter Day Crusade

In ancient days brave knights went forth
To fight the infidel,
Recover captured sacred lands
And seek the holy grail.

Today it's not for holy lands
On desert sands we quarrel.
Our sacred shrines are oil wells
Our holy grail a barrel.

Democracy in Action

In many lands disputed votes
Bring war as tensions mount
But in this blessed land of ours
We just sit down and count.

Of course it is a tedious task
Requiring lots of work
But if we want to trust our votes
It's one we dare not shirk.

So sharpen pencils volunteers
Put on the coffee pot.
We anxiously await the news
Did our man win or not?

Cross Purposes

We have to trim the deficit
Both parties now agree.
And then we need a tax cut too.
Why can they not see
These two are incompatible
Like driving to the lake
With one foot firmly on the gas
The other on the brake.

Bible Characters Re-visited

Cain

How could I know that if you struck a man
He might lie down and not wake up again?
I tried to wake him – wiped away the blood
And held him in my arms. I didn't know
A man could die just like a sheep or goat.
I was angry, yes, but not enough to kill,
And more at God than him. He scorned my gift,
As if a piece of reeking bloody meat
Was worth more than a golden sheaf of grain.
I worked as hard for mine. He only had
To sit out on the hills and tend his sheep.
I bent my back, first to prepare the soil,
Then plant, then cultivate, then cut the grain.
The best I had was not quite good enough,
And so I struck in anger – not to kill.
How could I know?

Joseph

What did I do to make them hate me so?
I've thought about it often all these years.
And now they're here, hungry and begging grain
And I've the power to spurn them, jail them, kill them,
Do unto them as they have done to me.
But somehow I've no wish to seek revenge.
I have two sons, and now I understand
How much a father's favor means to them,
How eagerly they count each smile, each frown,
Each word of commendation, each caress
As if collecting evidence to prove
Who's loved the most. I see how hurt could grow
First to resentment, then to bitter hate.

Was it my fault our father favored me?
No, but did I always have to be
So eager to accept, so arrogant?
That dream I had of bowing sheaves of wheat,
Why did I have to tell it? And that coat,
I could have thanked him, folded it away
To wear on special days, not flaunted it
A daily insult to their jealous eyes.
But I was young. I didn't understand.

I realize now how much my foolish pride
Inflamed their anger and their jealousy.
Now God has given us this blessed chance
To heal our wounds, be brothers once again
And I forgive, for He has changed my heart
What they meant for evil God has turned to good.

Lot

It was too much to ask – not to look back.
What woman ever left the home she loved
Without a backward glance – one last farewell?
It wasn't that she didn't want to leave,
But something of herself still lingered there
Among the dusty ashes of the hearth
That baked the daily bread – the village well,
The sunny courtyard where the children played,
The rooms where she performed day after day
The hundred homely duties bound with dreams
That shape a woman's life. Was it a sin
Just to look back? It was too much to ask.

Job

They came again today to comfort me.
Cold comfort – to be told that all my woe
Is punishment for some dark secret sin.
In other words, I've brought this on myself.
Perhaps they're right, and all our troubles here
Are the chastisement of an angry God.
We've done enough to anger him, no doubt.

I'd almost rather think that bliss and pain
Are dealt to just and unjust men alike
By the indifferent, even hand of fate,
And the God we love knows all the grief we bear
And loves us still, and hears our faintest prayer,
And shares our joy, and wipes away our tears,
And walks beside us when the way is dark.

But this is heresy. They'll tell me so.
When they come back again, what shall I say?

Innkeeper

They say I turned them out. It isn't true.
I offered them the only place I had.
It was a busy time. The inn was full.
Already I had given up my bed,
And strangers shared their rooms, and some were
Glad to find a place to stretch out on the floor.

Yes, I remember them. They came in late,
And weary from the road, and she with child.
My heart went out to them. What could I do?
I treat my guests alike. There was no room
Even for a king if one should come.

But as they turned away it came to me.
There was the stable, warm with cattle's breath
And soft with hay. And they were grateful too.

And now I hear the baby born that night
Became a famous teacher. People come
From miles around to listen and be healed.
Some even say he is the promised king,
And yet he has no home to call his own
And walks and talks with common folk. Well then
He would not have scorned his humble bed
Or wished me to displace another guest.

I sometimes think – suppose he came again.
Would I know him, offer him my best?
And would he graciously accept the gift –
Sit at my table, share my loaf of bread
And talk – and would I listen and be healed?

Ruth

"She stood in tears amid the alien corn."

— Keats

I said I'd follow her. I've no regrets.
We share our sorrow. She has lost a son
And I a husband. She has been so kind
And treated me as if I were her own.
I must not let her know some of my tears
Are for the home I loved, my kinfolks there.
In daytime when there's work I can forget
But when the sun goes down I think of home
And when I sleep I'm there again in dreams.
I'll do my best to wear a cheerful face
And care for her, and never let her know.

Naomi

I never should have let her come with me.
I know she's homesick though she hides it well.
Sometimes I see her gazing toward the east
With such a look of longing in her eyes
It breaks my heart. I see how hard she works
To earn a meager living for us both.
There's nothing for her here – no friends, no kin.
She needs a husband and a family
To share the love she lavishes on me.
I'll do my best to make her happy here
And pray God will reward her faithfulness.

Elder Brother

He's back, and I'm expected to rejoice
Welcome him, embrace him, love, forgive
Forget the way he broke our father's heart
And brought disgrace upon the family name.

While he was wasting his inheritance
On wanton living in a far off land
I stayed at home and served my father well
And yet he never killed a calf for me
Or even thanked me for my faithfulness.

I saw my father wait day after day
For his return, or any word of him
Until he finally gave up all hope
And mourned as if he'd had news of his death.

And now he begs me to come in and join
The celebration, treat him like a prince.
I cannot do it. It's too much to ask.

Thomas

I was the doubter, but the others had
Their reservations too. I spoke my doubts
And He did not condemn. An honest doubt
For Him was worth more than a wavering faith
That harbors secret doubts, and covers them
With pious platitudes. For me a faith
That dares not question is not faith at all.

And doubt can be the growing end of faith
That reaches out, bears fruit, strikes down deep roots
That hold it fast against the storms of life.
My faith is strong because I dared to doubt.

Martha

How can she sit there gazing up at him
When there is work to do? I only asked
For help, and he praised her and chastised me.
I so much wanted everything to be
Perfect for our guest – the floor clean swept,
The linen spotless white, the food well-cooked.
There would be time for talk when all are served.

But now I'm hot and tired and in no mood
To listen to his words, however wise.
She plays the perfect hostess, calm, serene
While I do all the work. It isn't fair.

Mary

How can she fuss so for a simple meal?
He didn't come to feast. He came to share
His wisdom and enjoy our company.
He does not care for tidy housekeeping
Or table set with choicest food and drink.
He would be satisfied with bread and wine.

I know she's angry. And he made it worse
By praising me. Oh why can she not see
That listening is hospitality?
A courtesy we give our honored guest
Far better than swept floors and table set.

I'll make it up to her. I'll do my share
And more of chores tomorrow, not today.

Shepherd A.D. 30

They saw a star, they said. I saw it too.
But often on these clear, cold winter nights
The stars appear on fire. They heard a song
Of angels. Well, sometimes the loneliness
Out on these hills makes one imagine things,
And sounds that drift up from the town below
Blend with the wind to sound almost like song.

They had to go and find the newborn king.
I too had heard tales of a Messiah
But never had much faith in prophecy.
And so they went. I stayed to tend my flock.

But now I know He was the king they sought,
For I have seen His face and heard Him speak.
I could have been the first to welcome Him,
But on that shining night long years ago
I chose to stay behind and watch my sheep.

Peter

I said I'd follow him till death, and here I am
Peter, the rock, the coward, traitor, liar.
Peter, the one who never lacked for words.
What happened then? What devil held my tongue?

I only had to say, "I knew him well.
Of course. He was my friend." And now he's gone
And no one left to carry on his work
But me. Can I unlock this stubborn tongue?
Will there be time enough to make amends?

Roman Soldier

A crucifixion on the hill today
Unpleasant task, but we must keep the law
See justice done in this unruly land.
Two thieves who no doubt well deserved to die
And in between them was the strangest man.
They say he was the leader of some cult.
We have enough of those in this strange place.
He seemed a harmless sort, and yet they said
His crime was treason – claim to be a king.
If not a king, at least he was a man
The calmest, bravest I have ever seen
Facing a slow and agonizing death.
And as he died he said the strangest thing,
"Forgive them for they know not what they do."

After Thoughts

"Seek and Ye Shall Find"

"And He gave them their request, but sent
leanness into their souls."

— Psalm 106:15

Forgive us, Lord, our sins. And when that's done
Forgive the petty virtues that we boast,
The errors that strew wreckage in our lives,
Then, Lord, forgive us for the things we value most.

You spread your gifts like jewels at our feet,
The daily miracles of love and friends,
Of children's laughter, music, sun and stars,
We pass them by pursuing our own ends.

We ask, we seek, we knock and wonder why
We find no joy, but emptiness instead
Forgetting that our God is faithful still
But we have asked for stones instead of bread.

Conversion

Paul, light struck, fell blinded to his knees
And we who follow him still hope to find
Dramatic demonstration of God's grace
A flash of light, a miracle, a sign.

Is there no place then for a quieter faith?
More like the gentle coming of the dawn
That slowly rolls the morning mists away
And rims the sullen clouds with liquid fire
Till all the world is bright.

Or like the quiet glow from many lamps
That fills a darkened room
Till every corner is alive with light.

We seek a miracle on some Damascus road
When all the time within the Father's house
The lamps are lit, the table set, the hearth aglow,
The door ajar. We've only to come in.

Ultimatum

Join hands. The world has grown too small for strife.
It is too late to quarrel. Time and change
Have taught at last that we are brothers here.
We live together on this fragile earth.
Join hands and tend it well. Make peace, or die.

"And Bear Ye One Another's Burdens"

No one can know the burden
That another bears
With quiet grace
Or see the secret cloak
Of sorrow that he wears
With smiling face.

The hidden wounded walk among us
Every day
And if someone should stumble
Underneath the load
And lose the way
Judge kindly, neighbor,
Stoop to lift his burden
Share his pain
And set his feet
Upon the path again.

Twentieth Century Re-awakening

We closed the gates of heaven long ago,
With scientific fact, cut one by one
The gentle ties of mystery and faith
That bound us close about the throne of God.

Thought we were better for it – more mature,
More scientific, self-sufficient, more secure,
Free from all superstition, guilt and fear.

But now at times we almost seem to hear
Once more, as men of old, the voice of God
From some dry bush aflame, and feel again
In the cold dark the brush of angels' wings.

Motes and Beams

The faults of others are so plain.
It's strange they do not see
Their many shortcomings and flaws
So obvious to me.

But then there comes a sobering thought.
Could it be that I possess
Some fault that quite unknown to me
Might cause a friend distress?

I've learned to suspend judgment.
Before I air my views
Of someone's flaws and foibles
I'll try walking in his shoes.

"Let Him Who Is Without Sin"

It never ceases to amaze
How people dare to cast
Stones of criticism from
Their houses made of glass.

Confession

"We have left undone ... ."

— Margaret Sangster

I've no dramatic sins to bring to Thee
I've walked a narrow path throughout this day
But oh, the little things I could have done
To help another traveler on the way.

The word of sympathy I left unspoken
The gentle touch to show someone I care
The healing words to mend a bond that's broken
The soft reply when angry tempers flare.

The helping hands to lift another's load
The willing feet to walk the extra mile
The pause to help another on the road
To greet the stranger with a friendly smile.

This is my prayer at setting of the sun
Forgive me for the little things undone.

Inspired by a poem in my mother's scrapbook.

Hidden Treasure

"No block of marble but it does not hide
The concept living in the artist's mind."

— Michelangelo

Only the sculptor's eye can see
The image hid in the stone.
Only the craftsman's ear can hear
The violin's sweet tone
Locked in the silent piece of wood
Waiting to be set free.

There is promise in every human soul
That only God can see
May we find grace to look beyond
Protective masks we wear
Look deeper in each human heart
And find what God sees there.

Fingerprints

The skeptic needs more evidence
More scientific proof
Before he will acknowledge
What others claim as truth.

Why should we doubt
When everywhere
From starry skies to lowly sod
No matter where we look we see
The fingerprints of God?

Higher Ground

When wandering all alone in valleys dark
Confused and lost, Thy way we do not see.
Lead us to higher ground that we may find
The path again that takes us home to Thee.

Acknowledgments

The author wishes to express her thanks to the editors
of the following publications in which these poems
first appeared:

Chatelaine: "Carpe Diem"
Covenant Companion: "Twentieth Century Re-Awakening,"
"Ultimatum," "And Bear Ye One Another's Burdens,"
and "Conversion"
Dreamseeker Magazine: "Lot," "Joseph," and "Thomas"
Perspectives: "Job"
Rochester Post-Bulletin: "Appreciation"
Saturday Evening Post: "The First Shall Be Last"
Selco Regional Anthology: "Latter Day Crusade," "Viewer
Discretion Advised," and "Ancient Wisdom Re-visited"

Special thanks to my daughter, Janet Panger,
who prepared the manuscript, my daughter, Marilyn
Thompson, for proofreading, my son-in-law, Ken
Panger, and his son, Erick Panger, and son-in-law,
Bruce Thompson, for technical assistance.

I will always be grateful for the involvement of
my daughter, Roberta Shorter, who discovered my
poems while on a visit years ago and worked tirelessly
to type and organize them in three-ring notebooks

for family members. Without her initiative this book might never have come to be.

Thanks also to Virginia Woodruff, publisher, of Artpacks, whose expertise, suggestions, and creativity have made possible the book that you hold in your hands.

— *Ann M. Schultz*

About the Author

Age 10

Ann has lived in Minnesota all of her life. She was born in Minneapolis in 1917, the middle child of three daughters of Raymond and Phyllis Gray. Her father was a teacher, her mother a homemaker.

After beginning piano at age eight and becoming discouraged because her older sister was already proficient, Ann took lessons on a borrowed violin from a teacher who came to the house. She then went on to study at the MacPhail School of Music for ten years. While in college she performed evenings and weekends at a restaurant with another violinist and a cellist.

Following graduation from the University of Minnesota, Ann taught high school English, geography, art, and music at Graceville for one year

before marrying Robert Schultz, also a teacher. Janet was born while Bob was teaching in Aitkin, and daughters, Roberta and Marilyn, while the family lived in Worthington.

After Bob was hired by the Rochester School District in 1948, Ann remained a homemaker and also joined the Rochester Symphony Orchestra. She continued to play violin in small groups until, at age 84, she had to stop because of advancing arthritis. Books have always been a love of Ann's. Beginning when her older daughters were in high school, she worked part-time at the Rochester Public Library and later, at the Methodist Kahler Nursing School Library.

Ann and her husband moved to Madonna Towers in 2000, where she remains following his death in 2004. She especially enjoys reading, involvement in a writers' group, and visits with family.